THE ENCHIRIDION

The Library of Liberal Arts
OSKAR PIEST, FOUNDER

THE ENCHIRIDION

EPICTETUS

Translated by

THOMAS W. HIGGINSON

with an introduction by

ALBERT SALOMON

The Library of Liberal Arts

published by

Macmillan Publishing Company
New York
Collier Macmillan Publishers
London

CONTENTS

· · · · · · · · · · · · · · · · ·

NOTE ON THE TEXT

The text of the second edition is a reprint of the first edition except for a few minor corrections in style, punctuation, and spelling, which have been revised to conform to current American usage.

The editorial staff of the publishers has added a few explanatory notes which are set in brackets and marked "Ed."

O.P.

INTRODUCTION

The little book by Epictetus called *Enchiridion* or "manual" has played a disproportionately large role in the rise of modern attitudes and modern philosophy. As soon as it had been translated into the vernacular languages, it became a bestseller among independent intellectuals, among anti-Christian thinkers, and among philosophers of a subjective cast. Montaigne had a copy of the *Enchiridion* among his books. Pascal violently rejected the megalomaniac pride of the Stoic philosopher. Frederick the Great carried the book with him on all campaigns. It was a source of inspiration and encouragement to Anthony, Earl of Shaftesbury, in the serious illness which ended only in his death; many pages of his diaries contain passages copied from the *Enchiridion*. It has been studied and widely quoted by Scottish philosophers like Francis Hutcheson, Adam Smith, and Adam Ferguson who valued Stoic moral philosophy for its reconciliation of social dependency and personal independence.

That there was a rebirth of Stoicism in the centuries of rebirth which marked the emergence of the modern age was not mere chance. Philosophical, moral, and social conditions of the time united to cause it. Roman Stoicism had been developed in times of despotism as a philosophy of lonely and courageous souls who had recognized the redeeming power of philosophical reason in all the moral and social purposes of life. Philosophy as a way of life makes men free. It is the last ditch stand of liberty in a world of servitude. Many elements in the new age led to thought which had structural affinity with Roman Stoicism. Modern times had created the independent thinker, the free intellectual in a secular civilization. Modern times had destroyed medieval liberties and had established the new despotism of the absolute state supported by ecclesiastical authority. Modern philosophies continued the basic trend in Stoicism in making the subjective consciousness the foundation of philosophy. The Stoic emphasis on moral problems was also appealing in an era of rapid transition when all the values which had previously been taken for granted were questioned and reconsidered.

While it is interesting to observe how varied were the effects produced by this small volume, this epitome of the Stoic system of moral philosophy, these effects seem still more remarkable when we consider that it was not intended to be a philosophical treatise on Stoicism for students. It was, rather, to be a guide for the advanced student of Stoicism to show him the best roads toward the goal of becoming a true philosopher. Thus Epictetus and his *Enchiridion* have a unique position in Roman Stoicism. Seneca and Marcus Aurelius had selected Stoic philosophy as the most adequate system for expressing their existential problems of independence, solitude, and history. In this enterprise, Seneca made tremendous strides toward the insights of social psychology as a by-product of his consciousness of decadence (in this he was close to Nietzsche), but he was not primarily concerned with the unity of the Stoic system. Marcus Aurelius changed the philosophical doctrine into the regimen of the lonesome ruler. In contrast to both, Epictetus was teaching Stoic philosophy as a doctrine and as a way of life. The *Enchiridion* is a summary of theoretical and applied Stoicism.

Epictetus was the son of a woman slave, born between 50 and 60 A.D. at Hieropolis in Phrygia. We do not know how he came to Rome. He was there as slave to one of Nero's distinguished freedmen who served as the Emperor's secretary. While still in service, Epictetus took courses with Musonius Rufus, the fashionable Stoic philosopher, who was impressed by the sincere and dynamic personality of the young slave and trained him to be a Stoic philosopher. Epictetus became a free man and began teaching philosophy on street corners, in the market, but he was not successful. During the rule of Domitian, Epictetus with many other philosophers was exiled from Rome, probably between 89 and 92 A.D. He went to Nicopolis, across Actium in Epirus, where he conducted his own school. He was so well regarded and highly esteemed that he established the reputation of the place as the town of Epictetus' school. Students came from Athens and Rome to attend his classes. Private citizens came to ask his advice and guidance. Some of his students returned to their homes to enter the traditional careers to which they were socially obligated. Others assumed the philosophic way of life in order to escape into the sphere of Stoic freedom.

Among the students was a young Roman, Flavius Arrian, who took courses at Nicopolis when Epictetus was already old. Flavius, who was born in 108 A.D., was one of the intimates of Hadrian, who made him consul in 130 A.D. He probably studied with Epictetus between the years 123 and 126 A.D. The informal philosophical talks which Epictetus had with his students fascinated him. Needless to say there were also systematic courses in the fields of philosophy. But it was the informal discourses which convinced Arrian that he had finally discovered a Stoic Socrates or a Stoic Diogenes, who was not merely teaching a doctrine, but also living the truth. Arrian recorded many of the discourses and informal conversations of Epictetus with his intimate students. He took them down in shorthand in order not to lose the ineffable liveliness, grace, and wit of the beloved teacher. Arrian retired into private life after the death of Hadrian in 138 A.D. and dedicated himself to his literary work. He published his notes on Epictetus' teaching under the title: *Discourses in Four Books*. The *Enchiridion,* which was also arranged by Arrian, is a brief summary of the basic ideas of Stoic philosophy and an introduction to the techniques required to transform Stoic philosophy into a way of life.

Thus we do not have any original writings of Epictetus. Like G. H. Mead in recent times, he was completely dedicated to the human and intellectual problems of his students. He left it for them to preserve what they considered to be the lasting message of the teacher. In contrast to Seneca and Marcus Aurelius, Epictetus had no subjective approach to the

Stoic doctrines. Moral philosophy was the center of his teaching, and epistemology was only instrumental. It is even permissible to say that he took physics or cosmology too lightly. If this is granted, we must admit that he is completely absorbed by the fundamentals of Stoic thought as presented in the *Enchiridion*. Epictetus' personality is totally integrated in the act of reasoning which establishes conformity with nature.

A remarkable difference between the *Discourses* and the *Enchiridion* should be mentioned. The *Discourses* are a living image of the teacher in action; they present the process of philosophizing, not the finished product. They show the enthusiastic and sober, the realistic and pathetic moralist in constantly changing perspectives determined by the changing students with their various concerns, problems, and questions; his teachings, his formulations, have direct reference to the various life situations in which the students should apply and practice the master's Stoic teaching. No human situation is omitted; as a guide to conduct, philosophy has relevance for all. Whether the students have to attend a dinner party, whether they are among competitors in a stadium or in a swimming pool, whether they have to present themselves at court or in an office, whether they are in the company of their mothers and sisters or of girl friends, in all human situations the philosopher knows the correct advice for the philosophical apprentice. Thus, in the *Discourses*, Arrian presents the unique individuality of the philosopher and of his applied moral method in living contact with various students in concrete situations. Epictetus as teacher anticipates very modern educational methods in his regard for the structure of situations and the changing perspectives in human relationships.

Nothing like this is revealed in the *Enchiridion*. Gone is the Stoic philosopher as living spirit. What remains is the living spirit of Stoicism. The *Enchiridion* is a manual for the combat officer. This analogy should be taken seriously. The Roman Stoics coined the formula: *Vivere militare!* (Life is being a soldier.) The student of philosophy is a private, the advancing Stoic is a non-commissioned officer, and the philosopher is the combat officer. For this reason all Roman Stoics apply metaphors and images derived from military life. Apprentice students of Stoicism are described as messengers, as scouts of God, as representatives of divine nature. The advancing student who is close to the goal of being a philosopher has the rank of an officer. He is already able to establish inner freedom and independence. He understands the basic Stoic truth of subjective consciousness, which is to distinguish what is in our power from what is not in our power. Not in our power are all the elements which constitute our environment, such as wealth, health, reputation, social prestige, power, the lives of those we love, and death. In our power are our thinking, our intentions, our desires, our decisions. These make it possible for us to control ourselves and to make of ourselves elements and parts of the universe of nature. This knowledge of ourselves makes us free in a world of dependencies. This superiority of our powers enables us to live in conformity with nature. The rational philosophy of control of Self and of adjustment to the Whole implies an asceticism of the emotional and the sensitive life. The philosopher must examine and control his passions, his love, his tenderness at all times in order always to be ready for the inevitable moment of farewell. The Stoics practiced a Jesuitism *avant la lettre*. They were able to live in the world as if they did not live in it. To the Stoic, life is a military camp, a play on the stage, a banquet to which we are invited. The *Enchiridion* briefly indicated the techniques which the philosopher should apply in acting well the diverse roles which God might assign to those whom he loves, the Stoic philosophers. From the rules of social conduct to the recommendations of sexual asceticism before marriage, and the method of true thinking, the advanced Stoic will find all principles of perfection and all precepts for realizing philosophical principles in his conduct in this tiny volume.

Thus the *Enchiridion* was liberating for all intellectuals who learned from it that there are philosophical ways of self-redemption. From its time, the secular thinker could feel jubilant because he was not in need of a divine grace. Epictetus had taught him that philosophical reason could make him free and that he was capable of redeeming himself by sound reasoning.

In the Stoic distinctions of personality and world, of I and mine, of subjective consciousness and the world of objects, of freedom and dependence, we find implicit the basic elements of modern philosophies of rationalism and of objective idealism or pantheism. For this reason there is a continuous renascence of Stoicism from Descartes, Grotius, and Bishop Butler, to Montesquieu, Adam Smith, and Kant. In this long development in modern times, the tiny *Enchiridion* of Epictetus played a remarkable part.

The translations of Epictetus and of all other Stoics had the widest effect on philosophers, theologians, and lay thinkers. They were studied by the clergy of the various Christian denominations, by the scientists who were striving for a natural religion, and by the independent philosophers who were eager to separate philosophy from religion. There were many outstanding bishops in the Catholic and Anglican Churches who were eager to transform the traditions of Roman Stoicism into Christian Stoicism. Among the Calvinistic denominations were many thinkers who were in sympathy with Stoic moral principles because of their praise of the austerity of life and of the control of passions. Likewise the adherents of natural religion were propagating Stoicism as the ideal pattern of universally valid and intelligible religion. Renascent Stoicism had three functions in the rise of the modern world. First, it reconciled Christian traditions to modern rationalistic philosophies; secondly, it established an ideal pattern of natural religion; and, thirdly, it opened the way for the autonomy of morals.

ALBERT SALOMON

THE NEW SCHOOL
  FOR SOCIAL RESEARCH
July, 1948

SELECTED BIBLIOGRAPHY

Epictetus: Life and Work

Arnim, Hans V., "Epictetos" in Pauli-Wissowa (ed), *Real-Encyclopaedie der classischen Altertumswissenschaft,* VI, col. 126-131.

Arnold, E. V., "Epictetus" in Hastings, *Encyclopedia of Religion and Ethics,* 1912. Vol. V, pp. 323, 324.

Bonhoeffer, A., *Epiktet und die Stoa.* Stuttgart, 1890.

————, *Ethik des Stoikers Epiktet.* Stuttgart, 1894.

————, *Epiktet und das Neue Testament.* Giessen, 1911.

Bruns, Ivo, *De schola Epicteti.* Kiel, 1897.

Bultmann, Rudolf, "Das religiöse Moment in der ethischen Unterweisung des Epiktets und das Neue Testament," *Zeitschrift für die neutestamentliche Wissenschaft und die Kunde des Urchristentums,* Vol. XIII, 1912; pp. 97-110; 177-191.

Colardeau, Th., *Etude sur Epictète.* Paris, 1903.

Hartmann, K., "Arrian und Epiktet," *Neue Jahrbücher für das klassische Altertum,* Vol. XV, 1905.

Jagu, Amand, *Epictète et Platon.* Paris, 1944.

Lagrange, M. J., "La philosophie religieuse d'Epictète et le Christianisme," *Revue Biblique,* Vol. IX, 1912; pp. 5-21, 192-212.

Oldfather, W. A., "Introduction" to *Epictetus,* "Loeb Classics," Vol. I.

Souilhé, J., "Introduction" to *Entretiens.* Paris, 1943.

Weber, Louis, La morale d'Epictète et les besoins présents de l'enseignement moral," *Revue de Métaphysique et de Morale,* 1905, pp. 830-858; 1906, pp. 342-360; 1907, pp. 327-347; 1909, pp. 203-236.

Main Works on Stoicism and Related Problems

Arnold, E. V., *Roman Stoicism.* Cambridge, E., 1911.

Bevan, E., *Stoics and Sceptics.* Oxford, 1913.

Brochard, V., *Etudes de philosophie ancienne et de philosophie moderne,* Paris, 1912.

Hicks, R. D., *Stoic and Epicurean.* New York, 1910.

Martha, C., *Les moralistes sur l'Empire Romain.* Paris, 1886.

Murray, Gilbert, *Stoic, Christian, Humanist.* London, 1940.

Robin, L., *La morale antique.* Paris, 1938, pp. 57, 130, 152, 167.

Wendland, Paul, *Philo und die cynisch-stoische Diatribe.* Berlin, 1895.

——, *Die hellenistische Kultur in ihren Beziehungen zum Judentum und Christentum.* Tübingen, 1912.

Zanta, L., *La renaissance du Stoicisme au XVIième siècle.* Paris, 1914.

Zeller, E., *The Stoics, Epicureans, and Sceptics.* London, 1892.

Influence of Stoicism

Busson, Henry, *La pensée religieuse Française de Charron à Pascal.* Paris, 1933. Chap. VIII: Stoiciens et Epicuriens, pp. 379-429.

Dilthey, Wilhelm, *Gesammelte Werke,* Vol. II. "Einfluss der Stoa auf die Ausbildung des natürlichen Systems der Geisteswissenschaften," pp. 153-162; "Anthropologie, Stoa und natürliches System im XVII. Jahrhundert," pp. 439-457.

Groethuysen, Bernard, *Philosophische Anthropologie.* München, 1928. (Chap. "Die römisch-griechische Lebensphilosophie.")

Rand, B., *The Life, Letters, etc. of Anthony, Earl of Shaftesbury.* London, 1900.

Saunders, Jason L., *Justus Lipsius. The Philosophy of Renaissance Stoicism.* New York, 1955.

Wenley, R. M., *Stoicism and Its Influence.* New York, 1927.

THE ENCHIRIDION

THE ENCHIRIDION

1

There are things which are within our power, and there are things which are beyond our power. Within our power are opinion, aim, desire, aversion, and, in one word, whatever affairs are our own. Beyond our power are body, property, reputation, office, and, in one word, whatever are not properly our own affairs.

Now the things within our power are by nature free, unrestricted, unhindered; but those beyond our power are weak, dependent, restricted, alien. Remember, then, that if you attribute freedom to things by nature dependent and take what belongs to others for your own, you will be hindered, you will lament, you will be disturbed, you will find fault both with gods and men. But if you take for your own only that which is your own and view what belongs to others just as it really is, then no one will ever compel you, no one will restrict you; you will find fault with no one, you will accuse no one, you will do nothing against your will; no one will hurt you, you will not have an enemy, nor will you suffer any harm.

Aiming, therefore, at such great things, remember that you must not allow yourself any inclination, however slight, toward the attainment of the others; but that you must entirely quit some of them, and for the present postpone the rest. But if you would have these, and possess power and wealth likewise, you may miss the latter in seeking the former; and you will certainly fail of that by which alone happiness and freedom are procured.

Seek at once, therefore, to be able to say to every unpleasing semblance, "You are but a semblance and by no means the real thing." And then examine it by those rules which you have; and first and chiefly by this: whether it concerns the things which are within our own power or those which are not; and if it concerns anything beyond our power, be prepared to say that it is nothing to you.

II

Remember that desire demands the attainment of that of which you are desirous; and aversion demands the avoidance of that to which you are averse; that he who fails of the object of his desires is disappointed; and he who incurs the object of his aversion is wretched. If, then, you shun only those undesirable things which you can control, you will never incur anything which you shun; but if you shun sickness, or death, or poverty, you will run the risk of wretchedness. Remove [the habit of] aversion, then, from all things that are not within our power, and apply it to things undesirable which are within our power. But for the present, altogether restrain desire; for if you desire any of the things not within our own power, you must necessarily be disappointed; and you are not yet secure of those which are within our power, and so are legitimate objects of desire. Where it is practically necessary for you to pursue or avoid anything, do even this with discretion and gentleness and moderation.

III

With regard to whatever objects either delight the mind or contribute to use or are tenderly beloved, remind yourself of what nature they are, beginning with the merest trifles: if you have a favorite cup, that it is but a cup of which you are fond—for thus, if it is broken, you can bear it: if you embrace your child or your wife, that you embrace a mortal—and thus, if either of them dies, you can bear it.

IV

When you set about any action, remind yourself of what nature the action is. If you are going to bathe, represent to yourself the incidents usual in the bath—some persons pouring out, others pushing in, others scolding, others pilfering. And thus you will more safely go about this action if you say to yourself, "I will now go to bathe and keep my own will in harmony with nature." And so with regard to every other action. For thus, if any impediment arises in bathing, you will be able to say, "It was not only to bathe that I desired, but to keep my will in harmony with nature; and I shall not keep it thus if I am out of humor at things that happen."

V

Men are disturbed not by things, but by the views which they take of things. Thus death is nothing terrible, else it would have appeared so to Socrates. But the terror consists in our notion of death, that it is terrible. When, therefore, we are hindered or disturbed, or grieved, let us never impute it to others, but to ourselves—that is, to our own views. It is the action of an uninstructed person to reproach others for his own misfortunes; of one entering upon instruction, to reproach himself; and one perfectly instructed, to reproach neither others nor himself.

VI

Be not elated at any excellence not your own. If a horse should be elated, and say, "I am handsome," it might be endurable. But when you are elated and say, "I have a handsome horse," know that you are elated only on the merit of the horse. What then is your own? The use of the phenomena of existence. So that when you are in harmony with nature in this respect, you will be elated with some reason; for you will be elated at some good of your own.

VII

As in a voyage, when the ship is at anchor, if you go on shore to get water, you may amuse yourself with picking up a shellfish or a truffle in your way, but your thoughts ought to be bent toward the ship, and perpetually attentive, lest the captain should call, and then you must leave all these things, that you may not have to be carried on board the vessel, bound like a sheep; thus likewise in life, if, instead of a truffle or shellfish, such a thing as a wife or a child be granted you, there is no objection; but if the captain calls, run to the ship, leave all these things, and never look behind. But if you are old, never go far from the ship, lest you should be missing when called for.

VIII

Demand not that events should happen as you wish; but wish them to happen as they do happen, and you will go on well.

IX

Sickness is an impediment to the body, but not to the will unless itself pleases. Lameness is an impediment to the leg, but not to the will; and say this to yourself with regard to everything that happens. For you will find it to be an impediment to something else, but not truly to yourself.

X

Upon every accident, remember to turn toward yourself and inquire what faculty you have for its use. If you encounter a handsome person, you will find continence the faculty needed; if pain, then fortitude; if reviling, then patience. And when thus habituated, the phenomena of existence will not overwhelm you.

XI

Never say of anything, "I have lost it," but, "I have restored it." Has your child died? It is restored. Has your wife died? She is restored. Has your estate been taken away? That likewise is restored. "But it was a bad man who took it." What is it to you by whose hands he who gave it has demanded it again? While he permits you to possess it, hold it as something not your own, as do travelers at an inn.

XII

If you would improve, lay aside such reasonings as these: "If I neglect my affairs, I shall not have a maintenance; if I do not punish my servant, he will be good for nothing." For it were better to die of hunger, exempt from grief and fear, than to live in affluence with perturbation; and it is better that your servant should be bad than you unhappy.

Begin therefore with little things. Is a little oil spilled or a little wine stolen? Say to yourself, "This is the price paid for peace and tranquillity; and nothing is to be had for nothing." And when you call your servant, consider that it is possible he may not come at your call; or, if he does, that he may not do what you wish. But it is not at all desirable for him, and very undesirable for you, that it should be in his power to cause you any disturbance.

XIII

If you would improve, be content to be thought foolish and dull with regard to externals. Do not desire to be thought to know anything; and though you should appear to others to be somebody, distrust yourself. For be assured, it is not easy at once to keep your will in harmony with nature and to secure externals; but while you are absorbed in the one, you must of necessity neglect the other.

XIV

If you wish your children and your wife and your friends to live forever, you are foolish, for you wish things to be in your power which are not so, and what belongs to others to be your own. So likewise, if you wish your servant to be without fault, you are foolish, for you wish vice not to be vice but something else. But if you wish not to be disappointed in your desires, that is in your own power. Exercise, therefore, what is in your power. A man's master is he who is able to confer or remove whatever that man seeks or shuns. Whoever then would be free, let him wish nothing, let him decline nothing, which depends on others; else he must necessarily be a slave.

XV

Remember that you must behave as at a banquet. Is anything brought round to you? Put out your hand and take a moderate share. Does it pass by you? Do not stop it. Is it not yet come? Do not yearn in desire toward it, but wait till it reaches you. So with regard to children, wife, office, riches; and you will some time or other be worthy to feast with the gods. And if you do not so much as take the things which are set before you, but are able even to forego them, then you will not only be worthy to feast with the gods, but to rule with them also. For, by thus doing, Diogenes and Heraclitus, and others like them, deservedly became divine, and were so recognized.

XVI

When you see anyone weeping for grief, either that his son has gone abroad or that he has suffered in his affairs, take care not to be overcome by the apparent evil, but discriminate and be ready to say, "What hurts this man is not this occurrence itself—for another man might not be hurt by it—but the view he chooses to take of it." As far as conversation goes, however, do not disdain to accommodate yourself to him and, if need be, to groan with him. Take heed, however, not to groan inwardly, too.

XVII

Remember that you are an actor in a drama of such sort as the Author chooses—if short, then in a short one; if long, then in a long one. If it be his pleasure that you should enact a poor man, or a cripple, or a ruler, or a private citizen, see that you act it well. For this is your business—to act well the given part, but to choose it belongs to another.

XVIII

When a raven happens to croak unluckily, be not over-come by appearances, but discriminate and say, "Nothing is portended to *me*, either to my paltry body, or property, or reputation, or children, or wife. But to *me* all portents are lucky if I will. For whatsoever happens, it belongs to me to derive advantage therefrom."

XIX

You can be unconquerable if you enter into no combat in which it is not in your own power to conquer. When, there-fore, you see anyone eminent in honors or power, or in high esteem on any other account, take heed not to be bewildered by appearances and to pronounce him happy; for if the es-sence of good consists in things within our own power, there will be no room for envy or emulation. But, for your part, do not desire to be a general, or a senator, or a consul, but to be free; and the only way to this is a disregard of things which lie not within our own power.

XX

Remember that it is not he who gives abuse or blows, who affronts, but the view we take of these things as insulting. When, therefore, anyone provokes you, be assured that it is your own opinion which provokes you. Try, therefore, in the first place, not to be bewildered by appearances. For if you once gain time and respite, you will more easily command yourself.

XXI

Let death and exile, and all other things which appear terrible, be daily before your eyes, but death chiefly; and you will never entertain an abject thought, nor too eagerly covet anything.

XXII

If you have an earnest desire toward philosophy, prepare yourself from the very first to have the multitude laugh and sneer, and say, "He is returned to us a philosopher all at once"; and, "Whence this supercilious look?" Now, for your part, do not have a supercilious look indeed, but keep steadily to those things which appear best to you, as one appointed by God to this particular station. For remember that, if you are persistent, those very persons who at first ridiculed will afterwards admire you. But if you are conquered by them, you will incur a double ridicule.

XXIII

If you ever happen to turn your attention to externals, for the pleasure of anyone, be assured that you have ruined your scheme of life. Be content, then, in everything, with being a philosopher; and if you wish to seem so likewise to anyone, appear so to yourself, and it will suffice you.

XXIV

Let not such considerations as these distress you: "I shall live in discredit and be nobody anywhere." For if discredit be an evil, you can no more be involved in evil through another than in baseness. Is it any business of yours, then, to get power or to be admitted to an entertainment? By no means. How then, after all, is this discredit? And how it is true that you will be nobody anywhere when you ought to be somebody in those things only which are within your own power, in which you may be of the greatest consequence? "But my friends will be unassisted." What do you mean by "unassisted"? They will not have money from you, nor will you make them Roman citizens. Who told you, then, that these are among the things within our own power, and not rather the affairs of others? And who can give to another the things which he himself has not? "Well, but get them, then, that we too may have a share." If I can get them with the preservation of my own honor and fidelity and self-respect, show me the way and I will get them; but if you require me to lose my own proper good, that you may gain what is no good, consider how unreasonable and foolish you are. Besides, which would you rather have, a sum of money or a faithful and honorable friend? Rather assist me, then, to gain this character than require me to do those things by which I may lose it. Well, but my country, say you, as far as depends upon me, will be unassisted. Here, again, what assistance is this you mean? It will not have porticos nor baths of your providing? And what signifies that? Why, neither does a smith provide it with shoes, nor a shoemaker with arms. It is enough if everyone fully performs his own proper business. And were you to supply it with another faithful and honorable citizen, would not he be of use to it? Yes. Therefore neither are you yourself useless to it. "What place, then," say you, "shall I hold in the state?" Whatever you can hold with the preservation of your fidelity and honor. But if, by desiring to be useful to that, you lose these, how can you serve your country when you have become faithless and shameless?

XXV

Is anyone preferred before you at an entertainment, or in courtesies, or in confidential intercourse? If these things are good, you ought to rejoice that he has them; and if they are evil, do not be grieved that you have them not. And remember that you cannot be permitted to rival others in externals without using the same means to obtain them. For how can he who will not haunt the door of any man, will not attend him, will not praise him, have an equal share with him who does these things? You are unjust, then, and unreasonable if you are unwilling to pay the price for which these things are sold, and would have them for nothing. For how much are lettuces sold? An obulus, for instance. If another, then, paying an obulus, takes the lettuces, and you, not paying it, go without them, do not imagine that he has gained any advantage over you. For as he has the lettuces, so you have the obulus which you did not give. So, in the present case, you have not been invited to such a person's entertainment because you have not paid him the price for which a supper is sold. It is sold for praise; it is sold for attendance. Give him, then, the value if it be for your advantage. But if you would at the same time not pay the one, and yet receive the other, you are unreasonable and foolish. Have you nothing, then, in place of the supper? Yes, indeed, you have—not to praise him whom you do not like to praise; not to bear the insolence of his lackeys.

XXVI

The will of nature may be learned from things upon which we are all agreed. As when our neighbor's boy has broken a cup, or the like, we are ready at once to say, "These are casualties that will happen"; be assured, then, that when your own cup is likewise broken, you ought to be affected just as when another's cup was broken. Now apply this to greater things. Is the child or wife of another dead? There is no one who would not say, "This is an accident of mortality." But if anyone's own child happens to die, it is immediately, "Alas! how wretched am I!" It should be always remembered how we are affected on hearing the same thing concerning others.

XXVII

As a mark [1] is not set up for the sake of missing the aim, so neither does the nature of evil exist in the world.

XXVIII

If a person had delivered up your body to some passer-by, you would certainly be angry. And do you feel no shame in delivering up your own mind to any reviler, to be disconcerted and confounded?

XXIX [2]

In every affair consider what precedes and what follows, and then undertake it. Otherwise you will begin with spirit, indeed, careless of the consequences, and when these are developed, you will shamefully desist. "I would conquer at the Olympic Games." But consider what precedes and what follows, and then, if it be for your advantage, engage in the affair. You must conform to rules, submit to a diet, refrain from dainties; exercise your body, whether you choose it or not, at a stated hour, in heat and cold; you must drink no cold water, and sometimes no wine—in a word, you must give yourself up to your trainer as to a physician. Then, in the combat, you may be thrown into a ditch, dislocate your arm, turn your ankle, swallow an abundance of dust, receive stripes [for negligence], and, after all, lose the victory. When you have reckoned up all this, if your inclination still holds, set about the combat. Otherwise, take notice, you will behave like children who sometimes play wrestlers, sometimes gladiators, sometimes blow a trumpet, and sometimes act a tragedy,

[1] Happiness, the effect of virtue, is the mark which God has set up for us to aim at. Our missing it is no work of His; nor so properly anything real, as a mere negative and failure of our own.

[2] [Chapter XV of the third book of the *Discourses*, which, with the exception of some very trifling differences, is the same as chapter XXIX of the *Enchiridion.*—Ed.]

when they happen to have seen and admired these shows. Thus you too will be at one time a wrestler, and another a gladiator; now a philosopher, now an orator; but nothing in earnest. Like an ape you mimic all you see, and one thing after another is sure to please you, but is out of favor as soon as it becomes familiar. For you have never entered upon anything considerately; nor after having surveyed and tested the whole matter, but carelessly, and with a halfway zeal. Thus some, when they have seen a philosopher and heard a man speaking like Euphrates [3]—though, indeed, who can speak like him?—have a mind to be philosophers, too. Consider first, man, what the matter is, and what your own nature is able to bear. If you would be a wrestler, consider your shoulders, your back, your thighs; for different persons are made for different things. Do you think that you can act as you do and be a philosopher, that you can eat, drink, be angry, be discontented, as you are now? You must watch, you must labor, you must get the better of certain appetites, must quit your acquaintances, be despised by your servant, be laughed at by those you meet; come off worse than others in everything—in offices, in honors, before tribunals. When you have fully considered all these things, approach, if you please —that is, if, by parting with them, you have a mind to purchase serenity, freedom, and tranquillity. If not, do not come hither; do not, like children, be now a philosopher, then a publican, then an orator, and then one of Caesar's officers. These things are not consistent. You must be one man, either good or bad. You must cultivate either your own reason or else externals; apply yourself either to things within or without you—that is, be either a philosopher or one of the mob.

XXX

Duties are universally measured by relations. Is a certain man your father? In this are implied taking care of him, sub-

---

[3] Euphrates was a philosopher of Syria, whose character is described, with the highest encomiums, by Pliny the Younger, *Letters* I. 10.

mitting to him in all things, patiently receiving his reproaches, his correction. But he is a bad father. Is your natural tie, then, to a *good* father? No, but to a father. Is a brother unjust? Well, preserve your own just relation toward him. Consider not what *he* does, but what *you* are to do to keep your own will in a state conformable to nature, for another cannot hurt you unless you please. You will then be hurt when you consent to be hurt. In this manner, therefore, if you accustom yourself to contemplate the relations of neighbor, citizen, commander, you can deduce from each the corresponding duties.

XXXI

Be assured that the essence of piety toward the gods lies in this—to form right opinions concerning them, as existing and as governing the universe justly and well. And fix yourself in this resolution, to obey them, and yield to them, and willingly follow them amidst all events, as being ruled by the most perfect wisdom. For thus you will never find fault with the gods, nor accuse them of neglecting you. And it is not possible for this to be affected in any other way than by withdrawing yourself from things which are not within our own power, and by making good or evil to consist only in those which are. For if you suppose any other things to be either good or evil, it is inevitable that, when you are disappointed of what you wish or incur what you would avoid, you should reproach and blame their authors. For every creature is naturally formed to flee and abhor things that appear hurtful and that which causes them; and to pursue and admire those which appear beneficial and that which causes them. It is impracticable, then, that one who supposes himself to be hurt should rejoice in the person who, as he thinks, hurts him, just as it is impossible to rejoice in the hurt itself. Hence, also, a father is reviled by his son when he does not impart the things which seem to be good; and this made Polynices and Eteocles [4] mutually enemies—that empire seemed good to both. On this account the husbandman reviles the gods; [and so do] the sailor, the merchant, or those who have lost wife or child. For where our interest is, there, too, is piety directed. So that whoever is careful to regulate his desires and aversions as he ought is thus made careful of piety likewise. But it also becomes incumbent on everyone to offer libations and sacrifices and first fruits, according to the customs of his country, purely, and not heedlessly nor negligently; not avariciously, nor yet extravagantly.

XXXII

When you have recourse to divination, remember that you know not what the event will be, and you come to learn it of the diviner; but of what nature it is you knew before coming; at least, if you are of philosophic mind. For if it is among the things not within our own power, it can by no means be either good or evil. Do not, therefore, bring with you to the diviner either desire or aversion—else you will approach him trembling—but first clearly understand that every event is indifferent and nothing to *you*, of whatever sort it may be; for it will be in your power to make a right use of it, and this no one can hinder. Then come with confidence to the gods as your counselors; and afterwards, when any counsel is given you, remember what counselors you have assumed, and whose advice you will neglect if you disobey. Come to divination as Socrates prescribed, in cases of which the whole consideration relates to the event, and in which no opportunities are afforded by reason or any other art to discover the matter in view. When, therefore, it is our duty to share the danger of a friend or of our country, we ought not to consult the oracle as to whether we shall share it with them or not. For though the diviner should forewarn you that the auspices are unfavorable, this means no more than

4 [The two inimical sons of Oedipus, who killed each other in battle.—Ed.]

that either death or mutilation or exile is portended. But we have reason within us; and it directs us, even with these hazards, to stand by our friend and our country. Attend, therefore, to the greater diviner, the Pythian God, who once cast out of the temple him who neglected to save his friend.[5]

XXXIII

Begin by prescribing to yourself some character and demeanor, such as you may preserve both alone and in company.

Be mostly silent, or speak merely what is needful, and in few words. We may, however, enter sparingly into discourse sometimes, when occasion calls for it; but let it not run on any of the common subjects, as gladiators, or horse races, or athletic champions, or food, or drink—the vulgar topics of conversation—and especially not on men, so as either to blame, or praise, or make comparisons. If you are able, then, by your own conversation, bring over that of your company to proper subjects; but if you happen to find yourself among strangers, be silent.

Let not your laughter be loud, frequent, or abundant.

Avoid taking oaths, if possible, altogether; at any rate, so far as you are able.

Avoid public and vulgar entertainments; but if ever an occasion calls you to them, keep your attention upon the stretch, that you may not imperceptibly slide into vulgarity. For be assured that if a person be ever so pure himself, yet, if his companion be corrupted, he who converses with him will be corrupted likewise.

Provide things relating to the body no further than absolute need requires, as meat, drink, clothing, house, retinue. But cut off everything that looks toward show and luxury.

5 [This refers to an anecdote given in full by Simplicius, in his commentary on this passage, of a man assaulted and killed on his way to consult the oracle, while his companion, deserting him, took refuge in the temple till cast out by the Deity.—Tr.]

Before marriage guard yourself with all your ability from unlawful intercourse with women; yet be not uncharitable or severe to those who are led into this, nor boast frequently that you yourself do otherwise.

If anyone tells you that a certain person speaks ill of you, do not make excuses about what is said of you, but answer: "He was ignorant of my other faults, else he would not have mentioned these alone."

It is not necessary for you to appear often at public spectacles; but if ever there is a proper occasion for you to be there, do not appear more solicitous for any other than for yourself—that is, wish things to be only just as they are, and only the best man to win; for thus nothing will go against you. But abstain entirely from acclamations and derision and violent emotions. And when you come away, do not discourse a great deal on what has passed and what contributes nothing to your own amendment. For it would appear by such discourse that you were dazzled by the show.

Be not prompt or ready to attend private recitations; but if you do attend, preserve your gravity and dignity, and yet avoid making yourself disagreeable.

When you are going to confer with anyone, and especially with one who seems your superior, represent to yourself how Socrates or Zeno [6] would behave in such a case, and you will not be at a loss to meet properly whatever may occur.

When you are going before anyone in power, fancy to yourself that you may not find him at home, that you may be shut out, that the doors may not be opened to you, that he may not notice you. If, with all this, it be your duty to go, bear what happens and never say to yourself, "It was not worth so much"; for this is vulgar, and like a man bewildered by externals.

In company, avoid a frequent and excessive mention of your own actions and dangers. For however agreeable it may be to yourself to allude to the risks you have run, it is not

[6] [Reference is to Zeno of Cyprus (335–263 B.C.), the founder of the Stoic school.—Ed.]

equally agreeable to others to hear your adventures. Avoid likewise an endeavor to excite laughter, for this may readily slide you into vulgarity, and, besides, may be apt to lower you in the esteem of your acquaintance. Approaches to indecent discourse are likewise dangerous. Therefore, when anything of this sort happens, use the first fit opportunity to rebuke him who makes advances that way, or, at least, by silence and blushing and a serious look show yourself to be displeased by such talk.

XXXIV

If you are dazzled by the semblance of any promised pleasure, guard yourself against being bewildered by it; but let the affair wait your leisure, and procure yourself some delay. Then bring to your mind both points of time—that in which you shall enjoy the pleasure, and that in which you will repent and reproach yourself, after you have enjoyed it—and set before you, in opposition to these, how you will rejoice and applaud yourself if you abstain. And even though it should appear to you a seasonable gratification, take heed that its enticements and allurements and seductions may not subdue you, but set in opposition to this how much better it is to be conscious of having gained so great a victory.

XXXV

When you do anything from a clear judgment that it ought to be done, never shrink from being seen to do it, even though the world should misunderstand it; for if you are not acting rightly, shun the action itself; if you are, why fear those who wrongly censure you?

XXXVI

As the proposition, "either it is day or it is night," has much force in a disjunctive argument, but none at all in a conjunctive one, so, at a feast, to choose the largest share is very suitable to the bodily appetite, but utterly inconsistent with the social spirit of the entertainment. Remember, then, when you eat with another, not only the value to the body of those things which are set before you, but also the value of proper courtesy toward your host.

XXXVII

If you have assumed any character beyond your strength, you have both demeaned yourself ill in that and quitted one which you might have supported.

XXXVIII

As in walking you take care not to tread upon a nail, or turn your foot, so likewise take care not to hurt the ruling faculty of your mind. And if we were to guard against this in every action, we should enter upon action more safely.

XXXIX

The body is to everyone the proper measure of its possessions, as the foot is of the shoe. If, therefore, you stop at this, you will keep the measure; but if you move beyond it, you must necessarily be carried forward, as down a precipice; as in the case of a shoe, if you go beyond its fitness to the foot, it comes first to be gilded, then purple, and then studded with jewels. For to that which once exceeds the fit measure there is no bound.

XL

Women from fourteen years old are flattered by men with the title of mistresses. Therefore, perceiving that they are regarded only as qualified to give men pleasure, they begin to adorn themselves, and in that to place all their hopes. It is worth while, therefore, to try that they may perceive themselves honored only so far as they appear beautiful in their demeanor and modestly virtuous.

XLI

It is a mark of want of intellect to spend much time in things relating to the body, as to be immoderate in exercises, in eating and drinking, and in the discharge of other animal functions. These things should be done incidentally and our main strength be applied to our reason.

XLII

When any person does ill by you, or speaks ill of you, remember that he acts or speaks from an impression that it is right for him to do so. Now it is not possible that he should follow what appears right to you, but only what appears so to himself. Therefore, if he judges from false appearances, he is the person hurt, since he, too, is the person deceived. For if anyone takes a true proposition to be false, the proposition is not hurt, but only the man is deceived. Setting out, then, from these principles, you will meekly bear with a person who reviles you, for you will say upon every occasion, "It seemed so to him."

XLIII

Everything has two handles: one by which it may be borne, another by which it cannot. If your brother acts unjustly, do not lay hold on the affair by the handle of his injustice, for by that it cannot be borne, but rather by the opposite—that he is your brother, that he was brought up with you; and thus you will lay hold on it as it is to be borne.

XLIV

These reasonings have no logical connection: "I am richer than you, therefore I am your superior." "I am more eloquent than you, therefore I am your superior." The true logical connection is rather this: "I am richer than you, therefore my possessions must exceed yours." "I am more eloquent than you, therefore my style must surpass yours." But you, after all, consist neither in property nor in style.

XLV

Does anyone bathe hastily? Do not say that he does it ill, but hastily. Does anyone drink much wine? Do not say that he does ill, but that he drinks a great deal. For unless you perfectly understand his motives, how should you know if he acts ill? Thus you will not risk yielding to any appearances but such as you fully comprehend.

XLVI

Never proclaim yourself a philosopher, nor make much talk among the ignorant about your principles, but show them by actions. Thus, at an entertainment, do not discourse how people ought to eat, but eat as you ought. For remember that thus Socrates also universally avoided all ostentation. And when persons came to him and desired to be introduced by him to philosophers, he took them and introduced them; so well did he bear being overlooked. So if ever there should be among the ignorant any discussion of principles, be for the most part silent. For there is great danger in hastily throwing out what is undigested. And if anyone tells you that you know nothing, and you are not nettled at it, then you may be sure that you have really entered on your work. For sheep do not hastily throw up the grass to show the shepherds how much they have eaten, but, inwardly digesting their food, they produce it outwardly in wool and milk. Thus, therefore, do you not make an exhibition before the ignorant of your principles, but of the actions to which their digestion gives rise.

XLVII

When you have learned to nourish your body frugally, do not pique yourself upon it; nor, if you drink water, be saying upon every occasion, "I drink water." But first consider how much more frugal are the poor than we, and how much more patient of hardship. If at any time you would inure yourself by exercise to labor and privation, for your own sake and not for the public, do not attempt great feats; but when you are violently thirsty, just rinse your mouth with water, and tell nobody.

XLVIII

The condition and characteristic of a vulgar person is that he never looks for either help or harm from himself, but only from externals. The condition and characteristic of a philosopher is that he looks to himself for all help or harm. The marks of a proficient are that he censures no one, praises no one, blames no one, accuses no one; says nothing concerning himself as being anybody or knowing anything. When he is in any instance hindered or restrained, he accuses himself; and if he is praised, he smiles to himself at the person who praises him; and if he is censured, he makes no defense. But he goes about with the caution of a convalescent, careful of interference with anything that is doing well but not yet quite secure. He restrains desire; he transfers his aversion to those things only which thwart the proper use of our own will; he employs his energies moderately in all directions; if he appears stupid or ignorant, he does not care; and, in a word, he keeps watch over himself as over an enemy and one in ambush.

XLIX

When anyone shows himself vain on being able to understand and interpret the works of Chrysippus,[7] say to yourself: "Unless Chrysippus had written obscurely, this person would have had nothing to be vain of. But what do I desire?

[7] [Chrysippus (c. 280–207 B.C.) was a Stoic philosopher who became head of the Stoa after Cleanthes. His works, which are lost, were most influential and were generally accepted as the authoritative interpretation of orthodox Stoic philosophy.—Ed.]

To understand nature, and follow her. I ask, then, who inter-
prets her; and hearing that Chrysippus does, I have recourse
to him. I do not understand his writings. I seek, therefore,
one to interpret *them.*" So far there is nothing to value my-
self upon. And when I find an interpreter, what remains is
to make use of his instructions. This alone is the valuable
thing. But if I admire merely the interpretation, what do I
become more than a grammarian, instead of a philosopher,
except, indeed, that instead of Homer I interpret Chrysippus?
When anyone, therefore, desires me to read Chrysippus to
him, I rather blush when I cannot exhibit actions that are
harmonious and consonant with his discourse.

L

Whatever rules you have adopted, abide by them as laws,
and as if you would be impious to transgress them; and do
not regard what anyone says of you, for this, after all, is no
concern of yours. How long, then, will you delay to demand
of yourself the noblest improvements, and in no instance to
transgress the judgments of reason? You have received the
philosophic principles with which you ought to be conversant;
and you have been conversant with them. For what other
master, then, do you wait as an excuse for this delay in self-
reformation? You are no longer a boy but a grown man. If,
therefore, you will be negligent and slothful, and always add
procrastination to procrastination, purpose to purpose, and
fix day after day in which you will attend to yourself, you
will insensibly continue to accomplish nothing and, living
and dying, remain of vulgar mind. This instant, then, think
yourself worthy of living as a man grown up and a proficient.
Let whatever appears to be the best be to you an inviolable
law. And if any instance of pain or pleasure, glory or disgrace,
be set before you, remember that now is the combat, now the
Olympiad comes on, nor can it be put off; and that by one
failure and defeat honor may be lost or—won. Thus Socrates
became perfect, improving himself by everything, following

reason alone. And though you are not yet a Socrates, you ought, however, to live as one seeking to be a Socrates.

LI

The first and most necessary topic in philosophy is the practical application of principles, as, *We ought not to lie;* the second is that of demonstrations as, *Why it is that we ought not to lie;* the third, that which gives strength and logical connection to the other two, as, *Why this is a demonstration.* For what is demonstration? What is a consequence? What a contradiction? What truth? What falsehood? The third point is then necessary on account of the second; and the second on account of the first. But the most necessary, and that whereon we ought to rest, is the first. But we do just the contrary. For we spend all our time on the third point and employ all our diligence about that, and entirely neglect the first. Therefore, at the same time that we lie, we are very ready to show how it is demonstrated that lying is wrong.

Upon all occasions we ought to have these maxims ready at hand:

Conduct me, Zeus, and thou, O Destiny,
Wherever your decrees have fixed my lot.
I follow cheerfully; and, did I not,
Wicked and wretched, I must follow still.[8]

Who'er yields properly to Fate is deemed
Wise among men, and knows the laws of Heaven.[9]

And this third:

"O Crito, if it thus pleases the gods, thus let it be." [10]
"Anytus and Melitus may kill me indeed; but hurt me they cannot." [11]

[8] Cleanthes, in Diogenes Laertius, quoted also by Seneca, *Epistle* 107.
[9] Euripides, Fragments.
[10] Plato, *Crito,* Chap. XVII.
[11] Plato, *Apology,* Chap. XVIII.